I0884158

BOOKWORMS

Animal Builders

A Spider's Web

Erika de Nijs

Cavendish Square
New York

Published in 2017 by Cavendish Square Publishing, LLC
243 5th Avenue, Suite 136, New York, NY 10016

First Edition

Website: cavendishsq.com

Library of Congress Cataloging-in-Publication Data

Names: de Nijs, Erika.
Title: A spider's web / Erika de Nijs.
Description: New York : Cavendish Square, 2017. | Series: Animal builders| Includes index.
Identifiers: ISBN 9781502620712 (pbk.) | ISBN 9781502620736 (library bound) | ISBN 9781502620729 (6 pack) | ISBN 9781502620743 (ebook)
Subjects: LCSH: Spiders--Juvenile literature.
Classification: LCC QL458.4 D38 2017 | DDC 595.4'4--dc23

Editorial Director: David McNamara
Editor: Fletcher Doyle
Copy Editor: Rebecca Rohan
Assistant Art Director: Amy Greenan
Designer: Stephanie Flecha
Production Coordinator: Karol Szymczuk
Photo Research: J8 Media

The photographs in this book are used by permission and through the courtesy of:
Photo credits: Cover Violart/Shutterstock.com; p. 5 Somyot Pattana/Shutterstock.com; p. 7 Mark Carthy/Shutterstock.com: p. 9 Brberrys/Shutterstock.com; p. 11 Schankz/Shutterstock.com; p. 13 Stefano Garau/Shutterstock.com; p. 15 Martha Davies/Storrs/iStockphoto.com; p. 17 Dave Montreuil/Shutterstock.com; p. 19 Xvazquez/File:Spider web Teruel.jpg/Wikimedia Commons; p. 21 Aleksandr Kurganov/Shutterstock.com.

Printed in the United States of America

Contents

Spiders make **silk**.
They spin it into webs.

Spiderwebs are strong.
They are also useful.

Some spiders wrap their eggs. They make a sac. This keeps the eggs safe.

Webs are for **hunting**.
Insects get stuck in webs.

Spiders wrap up **prey**.
This holds them for dinner.

Spiders can spin quickly.
Some make webs every day.

They eat the old silk.
They **recycle** the silk.

Some spiders nest in holes.
They make **funnel** webs.
Insects fall down the funnel.

Spiders are at home on their web.

New Words

funnel (FUH-nel) A pipe that is wide at the top and thin at the bottom.

hunting (HUHN-ting) Looking for something, usually food.

prey (PRAY) A creature hunted for food.

recycle (ree-SIGH-kul) To use something again.

silk (SILK) A thin, strong thread made by spiders and silkworms.

Index

About the Author

Erika de Nijs grew up in upstate New York and played college hockey. She is now a teacher and a writer who loves learning about nature.

About BOOKWORMS

Bookworms help independent readers gain reading confidence through high-frequency words, simple sentences, and strong picture/text support. Each book explores a concept that helps children relate what they read to the world they live in.